THE SECRET
To Calming Down

Written and Illustrated by Theresa Fontana

Written and Illustrations by Theresa Fontana
Edited by Vicky Shifley
Project Managed by Kevin Fontana

Dedicated to my Brockie Boy! May your passion fill this world with laughter and joy.

Back in the day I used to get crazy upset. My mind would race and I would even start to sweat.

Little did I know I owned secrets to my own toolbox.

My school psychologist shared the secrets with me in just a few of our talks.
THE SECRET
TO CALMING DOWN

They say it's easy to just calm down.

Relax.
You are fine.
Don't you frown.

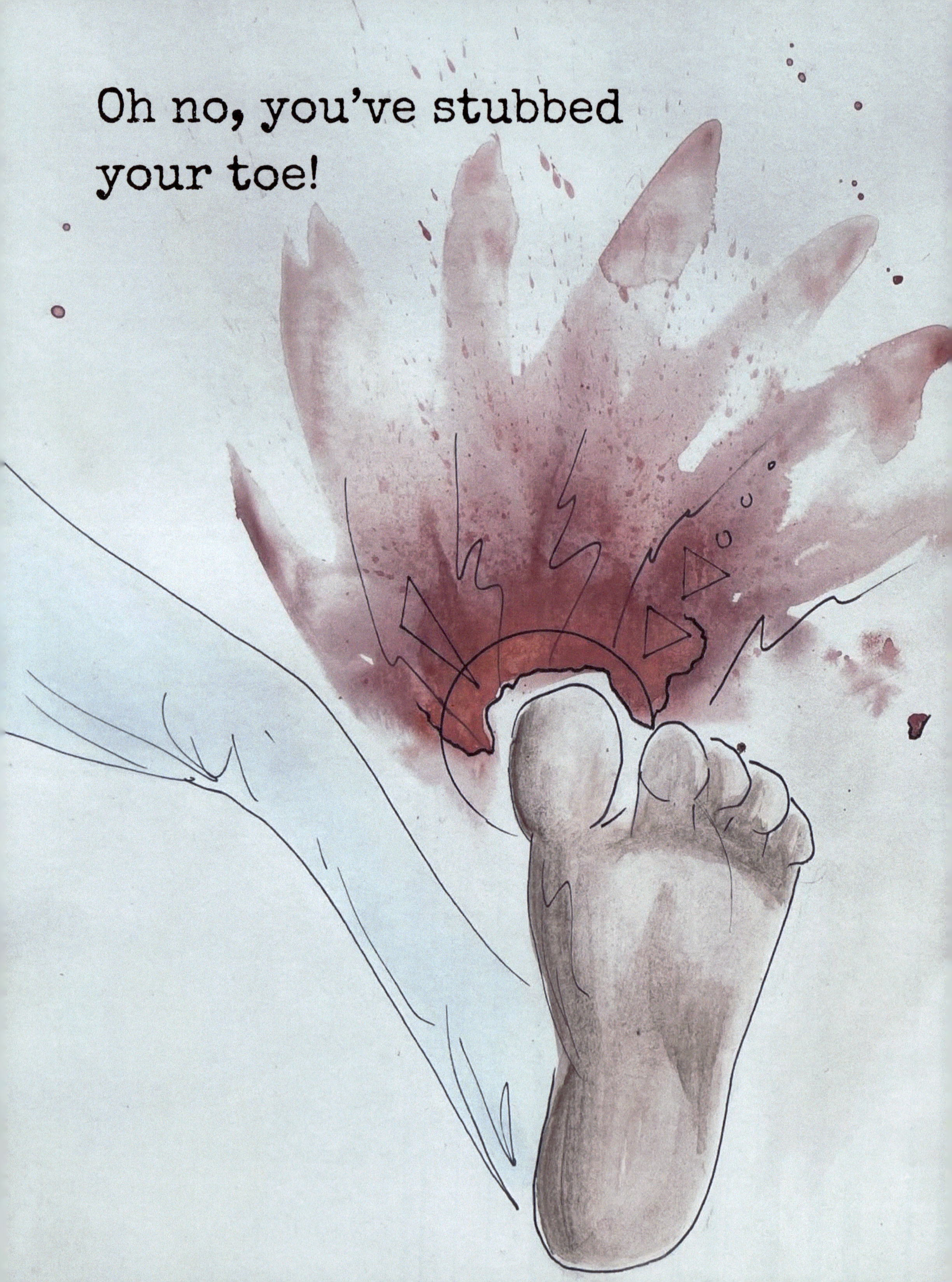

Oh no, you've stubbed your toe!

You just want to yell,
"Noooooo!"

Take a deep breath.
Count to 5.

I promise you,
you will survive.

Counting gives your mind
time to calm down.
The pain will go away and
so will your frown.

You get so upset you
lost the game.
How can you keep your
emotions tame?

Start by tapping each finger
and thumb
together

really

slow.

By the time you are
done, your emotions are
not such a show.

Hey!

You want to use
that toy she stole!

She makes you so mad.
You could hide
in a hole!

Pretend to smell flowers
and take a deep breath in.

Then pretend to
blow out
candles from
deep within.

Your turn will come soon.
Pass the time by
humming a tune.

When you do not want to share,
you tend to give a mad,
mean stare!

Instead try to offer a turn
to a friend. Making them
happy will make you feel
good in the end.

So the secret to calming down is just this.
Take a deep breath, count to 5, it's okay to feel sad, mad, or alive.

1 2 3 4 5
You can do it.
Take control.
Smell the
flowers, then
release and
blow.

Before you know it you will
be calm, cool, and
collected.

Neither you nor your
friends will be negatively
affected!

ABOUT THE AUTHOR

As a mom of three, elementary art teacher, and artist I write and illustrate helpful stories for children dealing with normal struggles. The secret to acceptance, calming down, taking care of a new pet, or even how to tap into their creative juices! How to fall asleep, be a good big sibling, or be a good sport! I write stories both my kids and students need, in a relatable voice, no matter what backgrounds, family dynamic, or cultures they come from. These child self-help books are all written in a format of a secret.

When my husband and I couldn't get our two year old to fall asleep, we started telling her stories we called, "Secrets." From there, the stories manifested into teaching our kids and my students about the world and tricks to being good humans. What kid wouldn't want to hear a new juicy secret?

This particular secret was inspired by mindfulness techniques. I learned the tricks from various professional development opportunities. They work for me and I hope they can help you too!

Check out www.TheresaFontana.com to stay connected, find out future book release updates, and access secret art lessons.